SAX

T0068441

PLAY BALLADS
With a Band

To access audio visit:
www.halleonard.com/myllbrary

Enter Code
2292-2971-1980-9711

ISBN 978-1-59615-797-2

EXCLUSIVELY DISTRIBUTED BY

Visit Hal Leonard Online at
www.halleonard.com

Contact Us:
Hal Leonard
7777 West Bluemound Road
Milwaukee, WI 53213
Email: info@halleonard.com

In Europe contact:
Hal Leonard Europe Limited
42 Wigmore Street
Marylebone, London, W1U 2RN
Email: info@halleonardeurope.com

In Australia contact:
Hal Leonard Australia Pty. Ltd.
4 Lentara Court
Cheltenham, Victoria, 3192 Australia
Email: info@halleonard.com.au

contents

Witchcraft...4

One for My Baby 6

Tenderly..9

The Christmas Song 10

After You've Gone 12

Manhattan..14

Why Don't You Do Right 16

I'm Glad There Is You 18

What a Diff'rence a Day Made.............................20

Sentimental Journey 22

ALTO SAXOPHONE

WITCHCRAFT

Carolyn Leigh and Cy Coleman
Arranged by Bob Wilber

5

ALTO SAXOPHONE

ONE FOR MY BABY
(And One More For The Road)

Johnny Mercer and Harold Arlen
Arranged by Bob Wilber

ALTO SAXOPHONE

TENDERLY

Jack Lawrence and Walter Gross
Arranged by Bob Wilber

TENDERLY
Jack Lawrence and Walter Gross

MMO 4105

ALTO SAXOPHONE

THE CHRISTMAS SONG

(Chestnuts Roasting On An Open Fire)

Mel Torme and Robert Wells
Arranged by Bob Wilber

THE CHRISTMAS SONG
Mel Torme and Robert Wells

ALTO SAXOPHONE

AFTER YOU'VE GONE

Henry Creamer and Turner Layton
Arranged by Bob Wilber

MMO 4105

ALTO SAXOPHONE

MANHATTAN

Richard Rodgers and Lorenz Hart
Arranged by Bob Wilber

MANHATTAN
Richard Rodgers and Lorenz Hart

MMO 4105

ALTO SAXOPHONE

WHY DON'T YOU DO RIGHT

Joe McCoy
Arranged by Bob Wilber

ALTO SAXOPHONE

I'M GLAD THERE IS YOU

Paul Madeira and Jimmy Dorsey
Arranged by Bob Wilber

I'M GLAD THERE IS YOU (In This World of Ordinary People)
Paul Madeira and Jimmy Dorsey
© 1941, 1942 (Renewed) MORLEY MUSIC CO.
This arrangement © 2008 MORLEY MUSIC CO.
All Rights Reserved

ALTO SAXOPHONE

WHAT A DIFF'RENCE A DAY MADE

Stanley Adams and Maria Grever
Arranged by Bob Wilber

WHAT A DIFF'RENCE A DAY MADE
Stanley Adams and Maria Grever
Copyright © 1934 by Edward B. Marks Music Company
Copyright Renewed and Assigned to Stanley Adams Music, Inc. and Grever Music Publishing S.A. De C.V.
This arrangement Copyright © 2008 by Stanley Adams Music, Inc. and Grever Music Publishing S.A. De C.V.
All Rights for Stanley Adams Music, Inc. Administered by The Songwriters Guild of America
All Rights for Grever Music Publishing S.A. De C.V. in the U.S. Administered by Universal Music Z-Tunes LLC
All Rights for the World Excluding U.S. Administered by Edward B. Marks Music Company
International Copyright Secured All Rights Reserved Used by Permission

ALTO SAXOPHONE

SENTIMENTAL JOURNEY

Bud Green, Les Brown and Ben Homer
Arranged by Bob Wilber

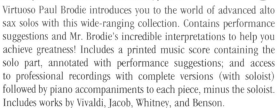

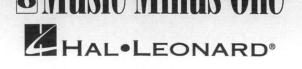